Courtship

and

Marriage

Courtship

and

Marriage

Rev. John A. O'Brien

Family Life Center Publications

This book by Fr. John A. O'Brien was originally published as part of a larger work entitled *Courtship and Marriage: Happiness in the Home*, by St. Anthony's Guild Press, in Patterson, NJ, in 1949. The original edition received the *Nihil obstat* from Bede Babo, O.S.B., Censor, and the *Imprimatur* from Thomas A. Boland, Bishop of Paterson. This 2003 edition by FAMILY LIFE CENTER PUBLICATIONS is an abridged and updated version.

ISBN: 0972757120
Library of Congress Control Number: 2003109676
Cover design and layout: Catherine Wood

Manufactured in the United States of America.

Acknowledgments

FAMILY LIFE CENTER PUBLICATIONS thanks the Franciscans of St. Anthony's Guild in Patterson, NJ, for granting us permission to publish this updated version of Fr. O'Brien's important work. We would like to thank Stephanie Wood for editing, revising, and updating this new edition. We gratefully acknowledge Catherine Wood for the cover design and text layout. We also express special gratitude to Karen Wood and Philip Cutajar for their invaluable proofreading assistance.

FAMILY LIFE CENTER PUBLICATIONS
22226 Westchester Blvd.
Port Charlotte, FL 33952
www.familylifecenter.net

Dedication

Dedicated with loving gratitude to the greatest advocate
of Christian married life in the 21st century:
Pope John Paul II

Contents

Foreword   9
Introduction   13

1. Practical Suggestions for Choosing a Partner   17

2. Putting Prudence into Practice
The Secret to Making a Choice You Won't Regret   29

3. Passion and Purity
Safeguarding a Priceless Treasure   41

Conclusion: The Supreme Achievement   53
Endnotes   54
Resources   55
About the Author   63

Foreword

I'm a baby boomer, one of those who entered my young adult years in the late 1960's. While attending a state university, I witnessed a sexual revolution that discarded Christian morality. Mine was the *Woodstock* generation. We were told that we were in the new Age of Aquarius where free love would prevail over repressive Christianity.

I was born the year before Fr. O'Brien's book was initially published. (No, you're not supposed to turn to the copyright page to look up the year.) By the time I entered college, I wouldn't have thought Fr. O'Brien's book was worth the price of a match to burn it. Surprisingly, here I am in the first few years of a new millennium eager to spend the scarce resources of a non-profit organization to make his work available to a new generation. Why? There are two reasons.

First, some unexpected outcomes of the sexual revolution changed my mind. Sexual liberation was anything but liberating. The free love revolution fueled abortion on demand, unparalleled rates of divorce, a worldwide AIDS epidemic, and millions of profoundly broken hearts.

At my first conference on *The ABCs of Choosing a Good Spouse*, I began my talk saying, "I'm here tonight because I am sick and tired of just passing the *Kleenex* box." I related stories of men and women sitting in my office weeping over their failed marriages. My personality is to be a "fixer;" I like to solve problems. Yet after many marital mistakes are made, it is often very difficult to fix them.

After three decades of passing the *Kleenex*, I figured that the new millennium was the time for a radical renewal of courtship and marriage. Most serious marriage problems can be prevented, starting with building a budding relationship on Christian morality.

I knew enough to avoid those foolhardy novelties promising to improve marriage. I wanted the real stuff. I wanted tried and true wisdom. I knew modern marriages needed a "Back to the Future" strategy. Through the gracious assistance of a research librarian at Christendom College and the kind staff at Loome Booksellers, I found an abundance of articles, journals, and books, including Fr. O'Brien's.

My second reason for republishing Fr. O'Brien's book relates to the contemporary moral memory loss. It seems as though our sexually revolutionized culture has clouded the vision of many loyal Catholics.

A few Catholic leaders have criticized the contemporary "hands-off & no-kissing" courtship recommendations by recent writers. I have joined with these writers in advocating the *voluntary* decision to abstain from physical expressions of affection until marriage. Yet one conservative Catholic periodical went to the extreme of calling such advice "Calvinism and not Catholicism."

Anyone taking the time to read respected Catholic moral theologians of just a generation ago would never make such an uninformed statement. Yet such statements highlight the contemporary need for Fr. O'Brien's book.

When it was initially published, this Notre Dame moral theology professor's book would not have raised any surprised eyebrows at his advice for courtship. Human nature hasn't changed, but our culture sure has.

Courtship and Marriage is a reliable guidebook, filled with practical advice, on how to preserve morality before marriage and thus provide the foundation for happiness in marriage.

If you seek lasting love in your marriage, then heed the advice in this book.

Stephen Wood
Feast of Maria Goretti, *virgin and martyr*
July 6, 2003

Introduction

I remember the first time I picked up the old 1949 version of Fr. O'Brien's book like it was yesterday. The worn dark green leather volume with mostly faded gold letters printed across the front opened to yellowing pages and that distinctive musty smell you find in old libraries and used bookshops.

It was the summer of 2001, and I was home from college and working for my dad at the Family Life Center. One of the first projects he assigned to me that summer was to read through Fr. O'Brien's book and then decide whether or not it was an appropriate work for Family Life Center Publications to edit and republish.

I was immediately distracted by Fr. O'Brien's old-fashioned, poetic style. *"Nobody writes like this anymore,"* I thought to myself in frustration. Not to mention his vocabulary! In the first few minutes alone I ran across several words that I didn't even know existed in the English language.

However, a surprising transformation quickly overtook me. I forgot about heady vocabulary and long-winded illustrations as I became engrossed in the truth of what Fr. O'Brien was conveying about relationships and marital love. My next thought shocked me: *"This sounds just like Dad!"*

My father has traveled literally thousands of miles, written hundreds of pages, and spoken countless hours to men and women around the world on topics relating to successful marriage and family life. For years he has challenged Christians with the principles of honorable courtship as an alternative to the failed twentieth century concept of recreational dating.

As I digested Fr. O'Brien's book, I came to realize that the advice he gave was the same wisdom I had received from my own father, who has spent most of his adult life striving to strengthen Christian marriages worldwide. While Dad has frequently been told that his courtship message is too radical for the present generation of young adults, I'm not convinced. It seems that the message of honorable courtship isn't so extreme after all – it's just the way relationships have always been conducted up until the last century.

Admittedly, many young adults in the modern world are afraid of the word "courtship." The majority of our generation still considers courtship to be an antiquated principle that might as well have sprung out of the Dark Ages.

But we're just starting to dance to a different tune. Those of us who've noticed that the dating practices of the past century didn't work – especially as we enter an adult society torn to shreds by divorce and fatherlessness – are starting to realize that maybe things worked better when they were done the "old fashioned" way: *God's* way.

I challenge you to read on with an open mind and a receptive heart. My hope is that you'll discover, like I did, that Fr. O'Brien's book isn't outdated, but right on target, and that honorable courtship is indeed the answer to a generation of broken homes and shattered hearts. And who knows? Fr. O'Brien's challenging words of wisdom just may be the very tool that will literally save *your* marriage...even before it begins.

Stephanie Wood

Practical Suggestions for Choosing a Partner

It is not good that the man should be alone;
I will make him a helper fit for him. – Genesis 2:18

Falling in love is an experience that comes to everyone. Usually it comes when one is at the threshold of young manhood or womanhood. The emotions which have been simmering during the teen years flame into raging love when a man singles out, from among all women, the sweetheart whom he hopes to win as his partner on the journey through life. The consequences of his choice will stretch to the end of life's journey — and beyond.

Because that choice is made while his emotions are pounding sledgehammer blows upon his heart, a man stands at that time in particular need of guidance. Emotions tend to disturb the even functioning of the mind. They speak a language of their own — the language of love. But into that language the voice of reason must creep and make itself heard. Love is proverbially blind. Only intelligence can give it sight.

Happy is the man who, while in love, still keeps his feet on the ground — with at least one ear attuned to the voice of reason.

A couple's eyes tend to rest contentedly on the beauty of each other's face, but it's crucial that they learn about the character and disposition of their future spouse, too. After all, a man and woman will spend the rest of their lives with the person whom they choose.

I'm not trying to throw cold water on love's dream. I want to see it come true. I want to see the radiant happiness of young lovers blossom into the mature love of husband and wife, and reach the crowning glory of fatherhood and motherhood. I want to see their castle of dreams materialize in the sanctuary of the Christian home, where love, peace and happiness abide. I want that home to be a little bit of heaven on earth, a foretaste of that eternal home where love abides and enraptures the soul.

How to make your dream of lasting love come true

How can your dream of lasting love come true? By heeding the advice and guidance of our holy Mother, the Church. She doesn't offer couples a merely theoretical message, but one laden with the rich experience of the centuries.

The Church has listened at the altar while millions of couples have pledged lifelong fidelity to each other. She has also listened to the stories of domestic tragedies, and has seen eyes heavy with tears. She has fought against the lust of kings in order to protect the sanctity of Christian marriage and the permanence of the Christian home. Better than any institution in the world, the Church can safely guide couples along that dangerous path, strewn with a thousand pitfalls, that leads to the threshold of a happy marriage and into the fireside of a Christian home.

Thus, the number-one rule for making your dream of love come true is: listen to the Church.

A primary cause of divorce

Pointing out that marriage is indissoluble except by death, the Church warns young people to guard against the factors that make for separation and divorce.

The Church recognizes that one of the chief causes of divorce is a couple's discovery, after marriage, that they aren't compatible partners. When the dreamland of their honeymoon has yielded to the realities of a workaday world, they begin to perceive what a blind man could have pointed out to them before: that they have little in common. They are very different in temperament and disposition. They differ in moral character and religious outlook. They vary in culture and tastes. The delicate bonds which spring from true friendship are lacking. Familiarity first loses its charm, then its interest. Boredom sets in, and finally yields to annoyance and argument. The divorce court has new grist for its mills.

The characteristics that matter most

Why don't couples perceive these facts before it's too late? Why do so many of them fail to explore *before* marriage those important qualities of mind and character without which any union rests only on the quicksand of impulsive attraction?

A man seeks to court a woman because of the texture and color of her skin, the radiance of her eyes, the contour of her face, and other superficial items. But it's character, disposition, intelligence, understanding, sympathy, and unselfishness that count towards happiness in the home and the permanence of the union — not outward appearances.

While beauty and good looks are not unimportant, the qualities of mind, heart and soul mentioned above are infinitely more valuable.

19

The coloring of the skin changes, beauty of complexion vanishes – but character remains. It grows in strength with the passing of the years. The man who seeks to build his conjugal happiness upon complexion and appearance, with scant attention to moral character and disposition, often finds out later that he has neglected to build a solid foundation. True happiness is seldom found in a fool's paradise.

The Church urges men and women to select a spouse with due regard to the important requirements for a happy and enduring union. She warns them in advance that they will pay a heavy penalty for negligence or rashness in this matter.

Before the Church admits candidates to the priesthood, She requires them to spend long years in training and discipline, meditating all the while on the seriousness of the step they contemplate. Yet Holy Orders imposes no obligation of greater duration than that assumed in matrimony. The consequences of both last until death. Therefore, shouldn't candidates for matrimony use at least a small measure of the care and consideration demanded of those who aspire to the priesthood?

Safeguards for making the most important decision of your life

The simple truth is that the voices of earth and heaven thunder in the ear of the person contemplating marriage: they beg him to make sure of the presence of those qualities of mind, heart, and soul which alone can guarantee lasting happiness in marriage. In every aspect of human life, the use of reason yields a rich premium, its neglect a heavy penalty. In no field, however, is the reward richer or the penalty heavier than in the choice of a marriage partner.

Prudence suggests that, before making so momentous a choice, the advice of parents and other sensible persons should be sought.

20

Before making a significant investment, a prudent person will secure the counsel of other parties who are better informed and more experienced than himself. While such counsel is by no means infallible, it at least greatly lessens the dangers involved. When a person is about to invest his whole life, with all its hopes of enduring happiness, shouldn't he at least consult wise and judicious counselors about the momentous choice he is considering?

The tendency of couples to confide in no one about their engagement, and to keep the whole affair a secret until just before the marriage, closes the door to many helpful influences which would at least lessen the danger of making an obviously unwise choice. A person never makes a decision that involves consequences of a more far-reaching character than those entailed in the selection of a marriage partner. Therefore, doesn't it follow that here, above all other places, a person should use all the prudence and common sense he possesses to ensure that he doesn't make a fatal error?

Don't throw reason overboard

Some of my readers may feel I'm over-emphasizing an obvious point. The sad fact is, however, that this truth, so readily admitted in theory, is frequently ignored in practice. Thousands upon thousands of the marriages that occur each year soon end up in the divorce courts. Why? Simply because people insist upon throwing reason overboard; they refuse to consider what's needed for a stable union and enduring happiness.

Therefore, I urge all men and women to use prudence and common sense, consult wise and judicious friends, explore the possibilities for compatibility in matters other than sentiment, and make sure of the character, disposition, reliability, and religious outlook of their prospective partner. If these practical steps were taken, the great majority of marriages bound for disaster would be avoided.

Practical suggestions

The *Religious Bulletin* of the University of Notre Dame offers the following suggestions regarding courtship and marriage:

1. Keep your head. Love is proverbially blind, but if possible, keep your head.

2. Lead a clean life. This should always be possible. The great aids to it are: a) Clean ideals — the Blessed Virgin Mary for womanhood, St. Joseph for manhood; b) Clean companionship, dictated by decent self-respect; c) The private vow of chastity made with your confessor's permission; d) An ardent attachment to the sacraments and prayer.

3. Learn frugality. The woman who has to be won by expensive presents is not worth winning. Let her love you for yourself. If you spoil her now you'll have to pay the bills later on. Frugality is an essential of marriage.

4. Seek counsel. Your parents may be pretty dumb in your eyes, but they know much more than you do about marriage. And your priest knows plenty about what wrecks marriage. Those who don't consult him before marriage are most likely to do so after it's too late.

5. Never confuse either infatuation or lust with love. Love implies reverence. A man or woman who does not command your respect is not worthy of you. Your own self-respect demands that you shun such company; and if you are lacking in self-respect, you are doomed to learn by bitter experience that lust is a terrible master.

6. Marry your own. Your Catholic faith is your greatest treasure. Protect that treasure by taking as your spouse one who loves the Faith and practices it as you do. This common faith constitutes a powerful reinforcement of your marriage vow. It serves as an anchor, helping you to weather the storms of life that are sure to come.

As a note of special advice to women, they also recommend:

7. Pay some attention to a man's ability as a breadwinner.

Food must be provided for a family to survive. The mortgage, insurance, and utility companies present their bills with terrifying regularity on the first of the month. No pay, no service. More important than dancing dexterity is the ability to make a living and to maintain a home. This means a willingness to work — and to keep on working when babies come and living expenses mount.

The danger of haste

One of the dangers which the Church warns against is that of excessive haste. Divorce court judges repeatedly say that a large percentage of the cases appearing before them are traceable to undue haste. When a man falls in love with a woman, infatuation, not love, comes at first sight. A whirlwind affair ends in an imprudent marriage. The couple awakes from the honeymoon to discover that they're as different from each other as night and day.

As a result of their observations, the Church insists that couples go through a pre-marital counseling process, such as a pre-Cana program, which will help the couple see their relationship from an objective perspective. Through pre-marital instruments such as FOCCUS (Facilitating Open Couple Communication, Understanding, & Study), the Church helps couples prudently prepare for marriage.

Pre-marital instruments enable a vast number of incompatible couples to discover their differences before they rush headlong into the marital contract, only to clutter up the docket of the divorce court later on. Thus, the Church seeks to safeguard marriage not only in its sacramental character, but also as an institution that plays a vital role in the welfare of human society.

The danger of delay

While the Church warns against courtships of undue brevity, She likewise counsels against those of excessive length. No hard-and-fast rule can be laid down determining the exact length of courtship. In general it should be of sufficient duration to allow a couple to get to know each other's character and disposition quite well. This can usually be done in a period ranging from six months to a year. Being a period of stress and strain in many respects, courtship should not be unduly prolonged. Persons who keep company for many years are without the sustaining influence of the sacrament of matrimony, and are exposed to much danger. A too-long-drawn-out courtship wears away the glamour and drives many promising romances onto the rocks.

The function of courtship is to help a man and woman get to know one another well enough to embark together on life's voyage. But where no such end is anticipated, courtship has little or no meaning. Courtship may be compared to a porch, over which people walk to reach the door of the home. What would one think of two people who entered the porch and proceeded to remain there indefinitely, as if unaware that it is intended not as the destination, but merely as the entrance to their proper home? Similar is the state of those who, having entered upon courtship, forget that it's not the end but merely the means to the end — the passageway leading to the great sacrament.

The simple fact is that a grievous injustice can be done to a young woman by monopolizing her attention for several years, depriving her of many other opportunities, and then, when her youthful charm has waned, walking out. It's neither chivalrous nor honorable. Neither is it fair or just. When courtship is being protracted to unseemly length, a woman's father should ask the man what his intentions are.

In America, we carry to extremes the idea that marriage is an affair that concerns only the two individuals involved. If parents are genuinely interested in the happiness of their daughter, why shouldn't they manifest that concern in an honest and effective manner? In some foreign countries, parents take a much more active part in assisting their children in the forming of suitable unions. They view the matter with less sentiment, perhaps, but with much more practical common sense. The time has come in America, with the divorce rate mounting higher than in any other country in the world except for Cuba, when parents and pastors must take an increasing interest in assisting young people in the successful solution to this most crucial problem — the choice of a partner for life.

Happiness is a social affair

In common with all mankind, young people are engaged in the endless quest for happiness. But happiness is not a private or a solitary affair. Suppose that we say to an individual, "Here is a million dollars. Go and buy happiness for yourself alone. You must not seek it, however, in the friendship and love of other people." We would be assigning him an end, but would be forbidding him the only effective means of achieving it. Why? Because happiness is a social affair. It's found in the esteem and friendship and love of others. Like the moon which shines by reflected light, happiness is found in the reflection of the sympathy, trust and affection of others. Wealth, knowledge and fame cannot adequately substitute for these wellsprings of joy, and hence cannot bring about true happiness.

Loneliness doesn't do the heart good

Among the worst miseries of life is that of unrelieved loneliness. To go home at night, only to find it empty of any person interested in your struggles, rejoicing in your achievements, softening the sting of defeat with sympathy and understanding, is to live in a darkened chamber unlit by the sunshine of friendship and love. Just as other forms of life deprived of the sun's rays wither and die, so human life, robbed of the sunshine of love and companionship, loses its zest and vigor. Love brightens the world of human existence with the warm sunshine of happiness.

Since love, courtship, and marriage are so often treated lightly and made the butt of so many jokes, it's worthwhile to point out that they are part of a divine plan. The first pages of the Bible make this clear to us. After Almighty God had created the universe and all living things, He placed man, the crowning glory of His creative power, in the Garden of Eden, and gave him dominion over all living creatures.

Sovereign of Paradise that he was, rich in material wealth and in the chaste beauty of nature's virgin landscape, man still felt, in spite of it all, a void and emptiness in his lonely heart. Then out of the heavens the voice of Almighty God is heard: "It is not good that the man should be alone; I will make him a helper fit for him" (Genesis 2:18).

A practical and spiritual safeguard

With those words uttered at the dawn of history, God created a helpmate to be a companion for man, a promoter of his happiness, a protector of his virtue. The sacrament of matrimony is, therefore, a great source of mutual consolation, since it safeguards the virtue of both men and women.

God's perfect gift to man

Thus, no human faculty kindles the flame of love that burns in the hearts of lovers; it's a spark of the Love that's eternal and divine. This is the gift which increased even the happiness found in the

Garden of Eden, and which still transforms for all of Adam's progeny the toil of life into a labor of love. It is God's perfect gift to man.

The sophistication of the twenty-first century hasn't rendered superfluous or out-of-date the warning of the Most High, uttered at the dawn of human history, "It is not good for man to be alone." That warning is of perennial timeliness to every generation, for it is based upon the unchanging hunger and the ceaseless questing of the human heart for love and happiness.

He who finds a wife finds a good thing, and obtains favor from the Lord. – Proverbs 18:22

Putting Prudence into Practice:
The Secret to Making a Choice You Won't Regret

The wisdom of a prudent man is to discern his way.
– Proverbs 14:8

Choosing a spouse is one of the most important decisions a man or woman will make in life. The consequences of that decision are momentous. To a large extent a person's happiness both here on earth and in eternity hinges on this choice. Since this decision is fraught with consequences of such a far-reaching character, it follows that it should be made with as much prudence and wisdom as possible.

Company-keeping (steady dating) and courtship have their justification only insofar as they assist men and women in making a wise choice. They have no other reason for existing. This eliminates any justification for the practice of merely recreational dating. Indeed, the whole social mingling of the sexes during adolescence has as its chief end the preparation and development of young people, so that they may choose a suitable partner in marriage.

For that reason, acquaintance and friendship between the sexes should be fairly extensive. Dances, sports and social events of various kinds are all designed to promote such friendships. Out of an abundance of such social contacts, you're more likely to discover a prospective partner than if the contacts were narrowly restricted.

Hence it is important for young people to avail themselves of the many opportunities which the Church and society provide for acquaintance with wholesome and congenial persons of the opposite sex. The failure to do so often deprives them of friendships which would mean much for their future happiness. Instead of deterring them from forming such wholesome friendships, parents should assist them in every prudent way.

Practical suggestions for the pre-courtship period

The whole period before courtship should be wisely employed for the widening of your circle of friends. Since courtship limits your interest to a single person, it shouldn't be undertaken when you aren't in a position to seriously consider marriage. This means that steady company-keeping (dating) is out of place for those of high school age. Even those in college will generally be wiser to wait until their junior or senior year before they restrict their interest to a single person.

How often have we seen a college freshman, smitten with "love at first sight," limit her dates to a single guy, only to have the romance fade in the senior year – leaving her high and dry. The years of your college life should provide a wide circle of friends. Out of those many friendships it's likely that one based upon similarity in taste, temperament and character will emerge and mature into married love.

In short, I say to those looking towards the horizon of marriage: Don't pull down the curtains prematurely on making friends. Don't get panicky. Keep your head. Take your time and look around. Meet many people of good reputation and character. Mingle and talk with them in a friendly and gracious manner. Explore their interests and learn something of their disposition and character. Then you'll be in a better position to choose intelligently.

Remember that marriage lasts for life. If you choose with haste, you are likely to regret it for the rest of your life. A marriage rushed into heedlessly often turns out to be a prison cell with iron bars that can't be broken. While love involves the heart and the emotions, the approval of reason is most important. No adequate substitute has ever been discovered for sober common sense.

When it's time for courtship

Courtship fulfills a special function. That function, a legitimate and important one, is to enable a couple to learn more about the qualities of each other's mind and heart and character, to explore areas of congeniality in taste, culture, disposition, and character, and to ascertain their fitness as partners in this most intimate and enduring union. That's no small job. Indeed, it's the most serious and important one they'll ever be called upon to undertake.

Before entering steady courtship, however, they should be reasonably sure of their compatibility and should be in a position where they can definitely plan to marry within a reasonable length of time. What would be the point of keeping steady company when the young man — say, a medical student — sees no possibility of assuming the obligations of matrimony for five or six years? Is it fair to monopolize a young woman's time during all those precious years, with the possibility that the romance may crumble at the end? The fact is that steady courtship involves grave responsibilities that should not be taken lightly.

Courtship should be preceded by wide and friendly mingling with others, by the attainment of an age sufficient to permit understanding of the tremendous responsibilities of marriage, and by the achievement of the financial resources necessary to establish and maintain a home. When these elements are lacking, a serious relationship is unwise. Instead of aiding young persons in making a wise choice of a life partner, it's more likely to handicap and defeat them. Premature steady courtship is like expecting June roses to blossom before spring has melted the snows and sleet of March.

Discretion outweighs valor: preserving chastity in courtship

Now we must consider the importance of the preservation of chastity during courtship, the dangers which threaten it, and the means suggested by human prudence and divine wisdom for its protection.

Courtship is a time of stress and strain. New emotions struggling for expression are beating an almost ceaseless tattoo upon the minds, hearts, and nerves of the couple. Cravings and urges rooted deep in the biological instincts of the race are clamoring for satisfaction. The proximity of a person of the opposite sex, a person who appeals to one's whole nature, tends, unless careful precautions are adopted, to add fuel to the flames of one's natural yearnings. Chastity will not survive unless a courageous and determined struggle is made.

We carry our precious treasure in jars of clay. That fragile material will be shattered if we needlessly expose it to the heavy blows of newly aroused passions. Prudence, discretion, and the avoidance of all unnecessary risks constitute the only strategy which will lead to victory in this battle. Here, an ounce of discretion is worth a ton of valor.

Our safety lies, not in stalking the enemy, but in flight. "Whoever loves danger," warns Sirach, "shall perish in it" (3:26). Later the writer sounds the same note of warning: "Whoever touches pitch will be defiled" (13:1). He who needlessly exposes himself to the danger of unchastity shall rarely, if ever, come out unscathed.

The forgotten virtue of the 21ˢᵗ century

It's important to remember that the virtue of chastity must not be curtailed during courtship. It binds the couple in love to be pure in thought, word, and deed with the same rigor with which it binds all mankind. It binds Protestants, Jews, non-churchgoing people and unbelievers just as truly as it binds Catholics. Despite a common misconception, courtship offers no release from the obligation to preserve one's innocence. The courtship period, above all times, is when vigilance is of the utmost importance.

Keep courtship on a high plane

One of the most important truths that needs to be driven home is this: *Keep your courtship on a high plane.* Never allow it to degenerate to the physical level. The tendency to emphasize the physical will sound the death knell for honor and respect. With these gone, true friendship is impossible.

In all the long history of humanity, lust, naked and unrestrained, has never failed to deform friendship and love into an orgy of passion – whose end is nausea, remorse, shame, bitterness, and suffering. Its lethal fangs will kill the noblest friendship and poison the purest love. When allowed free rein, it will never fail to transform the paradise in which lovers ought to dwell into a purgatory, if not a hell, on earth.

Explorers in the jungles of Africa report that one of the most dreaded dangers there is a certain poisonous insect. It steals upon its victim and, by a fast but noiseless movement of its wings, cools the skin, thus reducing sensitivity to the injection of deadly venom into the blood. It's the capacity to desensitize its victim, so that he puts up no defense, that makes this insect so greatly dreaded. It's the same with lust. It steals subtly upon an individual, disturbs his capacity for clear discernment and calm thinking, and tends to anesthetize the moral faculty. That's why lust is probably the most dangerous of all the foes that lie in ambush for the human soul.

It's true that, in all courtship, the physical element of sex is present. But it must be kept in the background. It must not be allowed to dominate the scene, to direct the thoughts and dictate the conduct of the couple.

God has made man male and female. Each possesses a different nature. These differences are both physical and psychological (emotional). These two natures, each incomplete in itself, find their completion in that sacred fusion which is achieved in matrimony. It's sufficient for a couple to know this without seeking to explore the physical basis of these differences.

Subordinating the physical element of your relationship

The elements which are to be explored in courtship are those of taste, mind, temperament, disposition and character. The purpose here is to discover as large an area of compatibility as possible in all these important fields of thought, conduct and life. Such bases of congeniality will endure when passion is largely spent. Instead of growing weaker with the years, these elements gain in strength, tenacity and expansiveness. Along with the love which has deepened with time, they hold the couple together – with tenderness, yes – but also with strength.

One of the evil consequences of allowing the physical expression of sex too great license is that it impedes the intelligent exploration of compatibility in other fields. It frustrates the cultivation of friendship in its deepest sense. Friendship of mind, heart and soul can develop only when the physical is subordinated to the spiritual.

Man is more than an animal. He is essentially a spiritual creature. It's the mind of man which constitutes his distinctive nature and his supreme glory. This, then, is the part of his nature which must be explored and cultivated if friendship is to find its anchorage in an enduring element. An attraction which springs largely from the physical element of sex is an insecure foundation for enduring friendship and conjugal love.

Follow a "hands-off" policy during courtship

Because of the explosive character of sex, which acts like dynamite when ignited by a fuse, the importance of restraining the physical element in courtship can scarcely be overstressed. The basic and all-important rule for all couples to remember is this:

Follow a "hands-off" policy during courtship. This is the wisest and the safest course. Respect the person of the friend with whom you are keeping company. Don't try to set him or her — and yourself as well — on fire. Why excite desires which can't be satisfied, save at the expense of all that you both hold dear? Why torture your friend? Why make him restless and uneasy? Why inflict upon her headaches and heartaches and, almost inevitably, a disturbed, if not an accusing, conscience? Isn't happiness, not pain, love's distinctive gift?

Genuine friendship doesn't lean upon the stimulation of the physical element of sex. It's injured and pained by such unseemly intrusions. Couples who are truly in love find untold happiness in each other's mere presence. You can have a world of good fun and clean enjoyment together without any appeal to lust. When couples keep their friendship on a high plane, precious qualities of mind, heart, and character never fail to unfold themselves like lustrous pearls. These scintillate and glow. Soon these strings of pearls will interlock. Mind meets mind, heart entwines with heart, and soul basks in the warm radiance of another soul.

When mind meets mind

Here is a friendship which grows from the entwining of the noblest elements in the nature of man. Such a friendship will reach its natural goal in the perfect fusion of two hearts and souls in matrimony. Those who keep their friendship on this high basis tap new fountains of innocent joy and laughter. A thousand times more satisfying and enduring than mere physical pleasures are those which arise from the contact of mind with mind, of heart with heart, of personality with personality.

In the personality of even the most prosaic individuals are hidden kingdoms of wondrous beauty. They won't be discovered through a mere superficial acquaintance, but only through patient exploration and continued search. Sometimes a smile in the face of defeat, a brave gesture when the chips are down, the manifestation of a determination to fight on against all odds to the unseen end, or a kind word of praise when sorely needed, act as a magic word opening doors to those hidden worlds of beauty and tenderness.

Know each other's differences

Here a word about the difference between the sexes is in order. The physical basis of the sex instinct is more highly localized in man and may be more easily aroused. In woman the emotional and psychological elements play a larger and more important role. Actions and contacts which leave her virtually undisturbed may greatly arouse the passions of her male companion. Consequently, it's necessary for the woman to bear in mind the wisdom of discouraging any liberty which may act as a fuse setting off an explosion on the part of her companion. In a sense, she must be the keeper of his conscience as well as of her own. She must be considerate of him as well as of herself. Yet how often that protection is denied a man, through her lack of understanding of his peril.

Not uncommonly, a woman fails to realize that a familiarity which seems to her to be an innocent expression of romantic love may quickly ignite the man's passion. Because the physical elements of sex are usually dormant or quiescent in her nature, she doesn't sense that what's safe for her may be extremely perilous for her companion. If these differences were more widely understood by both sexes, many dangers and temptations now unwittingly placed before men would be avoided.

"If each understood the other's nature and impulses better," observes Dr. J. M. Cooper, "their courtship problems would not, it is true, be solved one hundred percent, but there would be notably fewer slips, more mutual consideration and protection, less liberty, and more of ennobling and purifying love on its highest levels."[1]

A life preserver for men

The average man wants to do right. Under the influence of awakened sex instincts, however, he stands desperately in need of help. Even when outwardly pleading for liberties, he's often inwardly hoping and praying that the woman will save him from himself. If she is a wise and considerate woman, she won't fail to help him in his moment of desperate need. An earnest word, a look of disapproval, a sudden change in the conversation, a quick and determined step away, will be the life preserver thrown to him as he is sinking.

When he's rescued, with his senses restored, a sentiment of boundless admiration will well up in his heart for the woman who has saved him. That understanding gesture, in which sympathy is mingled with firmness, is the finest possible expression of true friendship and nobility of character. If a man has any streak of decency in him, he won't fail to take the cue and keep his courtship safely away from the danger zones from now on.

A curious paradox

Man is a curious paradox. This paradox asserts itself in a reaction which frequently mystifies women. Pleading and begging for certain liberties, he has perhaps obtained them. But does he feel pride over his success and gratitude to the woman who yielded to his entreaties? On the contrary, he's ashamed of himself and disillusioned with the woman. The contempt that he feels for himself spreads over to her who was the accessory to his misdeed. Instead of the exultant joy of victory, there's the sting of a humiliating defeat. The friendship has received a blow. If it's to survive, a different course must be pursued by both.

The man's reaction may appear strange and paradoxical to the woman. It may be all that and more. But it's as old as humanity. It's mirrored in the Second Book of Samuel, which tells how Amnon prevailed upon Tamar, much against her will. Did the action elicit his praise and ensure his love? Listen to the verse which immediately follows the record of the deed: "Then Amnon hated her with very great hatred; so that the hatred with which he hated her was greater than the love with which he had loved her. And Amnon said to her, 'Arise, be gone.'" (2 Samuel 13:15). This was the reaction of man at the beginning of human history. Such will be man's reaction till the end of time. For the spiritual element which constitutes man's distinctive nature will always rise in wrath and condemnation against the flesh which betrays him.

The feelings of nausea, shame and contempt after a yielding to temptation are not, however, peculiar to man. They're felt equally, if not to an even greater degree, by the woman. While she's not so susceptible to excitement through the physical stimuli of sex, she realizes that her maidenly modesty is her great treasure. From her male friend she covets, above all, respect and honor. When these are granted her, she knows that love will speak that nobler language wherein heart and mind will communicate sentiments, thoughts, feelings, and aspirations which lie too deep for words.

A woman is sensitive to the eloquence of restraint. She recognizes in it the expression of love tempered with reverence and esteem. A man will most surely win the heart of a woman if he acts always as a gentleman, and places her upon her rightful pedestal of unblemished innocence and queenly modesty.

A good wife who can find? She is far more precious than jewels. The heart of her husband trusts in her...She does him good, and not harm, all the days of her life. – Proverbs 31:10-12

Passion & Purity:
Safeguarding a Priceless Treasure

For this is the will of God, your sanctification: that you
abstain from immorality; that each one of you know how
to control his own body in holiness and honor.
- 1 Thessalonians 4:3-4

Unchastity is grievously wrong. Why? Because its evil lies in the use of a faculty apart from the purpose and plan of God and nature. The faculty of sex has been bestowed upon men and women primarily for the procreation of children. It's to be used, therefore, only within the framework of the family. When torn out of that context, it loses its meaning and its purpose. It constitutes an act against nature, an abuse of a noble faculty, and a violation of God's holy law. It becomes a mockery and a sham.

"Nor must we omit to remark," declares Pope Pius XI in his encyclical *On Christian Marriage*, "that, since the duty entrusted to parents for the good of their children is of such high dignity and of such great importance, every use of the faculty given by God for the procreation of new life is the right and privilege of the married state alone, by the law of God and of nature, and must be confined absolutely within the sacred limits of that state."[1]

"The law of nature" means the will of God as it's written in human nature itself. It binds all people at all times. Consequently, chastity is not a precept that is distinctively Catholic, Protestant or Jewish. It is distinctively human. By violating it, man surrenders the throne of reason to the instincts of his animal nature. In other words, he becomes a beast, even though he is camouflaged in the garb of a human being.

Why is unchastity such a grave sin?

The nature of sex consists of an intricate pattern of emotional, psychological, and physical elements, so closely interrelated and intermeshed that the arousal of the one almost immediately effects the stimulation of the other. One can't entertain an impure thought or imagination without exposing oneself to the almost instant danger of kindling the passions. Neither can one engage in an action which arouses the procreative faculty, without flooding one's mind almost instantly with thoughts, imaginations, and desires for further and continued pleasures of this kind.

Thus, either the thought alone, or the physical act alone, can act as a trigger for those primordial forces which move in the depths of our nature. They move along their appointed paths, and we don't chart those paths. They are determined for us by God and nature. Our responsibility lies in pulling the trigger which instantly throws these forces into action along predetermined lines. It's like flipping a switch that can throw a thousand-horsepower dynamo into action.

The pressing of a little button, the kindling of a tiny fuse, may seem in themselves to be actions of little consequence. However, they set off forces that give them enormous importance. Even a slender thought that edges its way, knife-like, into the mind is capable of setting off an explosion which will shake the very foundations of the human soul. Likewise, the least voluntary degree of sexual activity resembles the pressing of a button which, in turn, creates a force that is beyond our control.

Intelligent warfare

If we're to wage intelligent warfare against unchastity, we must know what the chief dangers are and how they can be overcome.

Failure to observe custody of the senses exposes one to many dangers. The suggestive story or smutty joke may start a train of thought which will be hard to stop. The lewd picture, the offensive movie, the impure novel, the risqué TV show, and Internet pornography penetrate beyond the retina of the eye to paint their images upon the mind. They're also likely to kindle desires and inflame passions which are not easily pushed aside.

Even when they don't immediately lead to satisfaction, such images implant the seeds of future action. They are like the time bombs dropped in the early years of World War II, which appeared to be duds. Crowds would gather around one. Suddenly, an hour after it had fallen, it would explode, killing great numbers of people.

Of all the senses, the eye is the one which presents perhaps the greatest danger. Custody of this sense is most important. It's not so much what one sees but what one looks at that matters. The follow-up of the visual stimulus with attention and eagerness, and with direction of thought, is what kindles the emotions and leads to a lustful act. Images etched deeply into the memory frequently serve as the hidden stimuli of repeated acts, and indefinitely carry on their train of evil consequences. One who really wishes to keep his chastity intact will guard his eyes with unrelenting vigilance, for through the eyes the Enemy usually seeks to gain entrance to the mind and heart.

The danger of physical intimacy during courtship

A great danger to chastity arises during courtship from the tendency to express affection for each other through physical actions. While this is a natural and universal tendency, it's also very dangerous. Caresses, embraces, kisses, and familiarities of all sorts may be well-intentioned, but they're loaded with dynamite. What begins as a mere expression of affection may quickly become charged with passion and change into lust.

While a few gentle expressions of affection may be without lust and carnal pleasure, and may seem innocent enough, the notorious fact is that they can easily and speedily degenerate into passion. The wiser and the safer course, then, is to follow the "hands-off" policy: to abstain from all physical contact. After engagement, it may be possible for the couple to express their love through a modest kiss or a reverent caress. Even here, however, great restraint and constant vigilance are in order — for the precept of chastity binds an engaged couple as it binds all the rest of mankind.

Exercise double caution during engagement

In fact, double caution would seem to be called for during engagement, because of the very fact that the couple loves each other so deeply and so strongly. They must always remember that they're not cold white marble, but flesh and blood with an age-old record of weakness. Hold straw before a flame and it will burn. If couples are not to sear their consciences, they must keep away from situations in which spontaneous combustion could easily occur. Let such an engaged couple remember that their marital love will be all the sweeter because of the restraint they exercise during the days of their courtship.

The number-one enemy of courtship

A danger which threatens the observance of the rule just mentioned is an empty home, apartment, or parked car. These places have spelled misery, headache, heartache, ruin and even tragedy for countless thousands of couples. Authorities in all parts of the nation have branded these unmonitored places "enemy number-one" to the chastity of courting men and women.

With the twin cloaks of darkness and seclusion thrown around them, a couple parked along a quiet street or alone in an apartment are deliberately subjecting their virtue to great and needless strain. They're courting disaster, not love. Let all courting couples avoid the parked car or the empty apartment as they would a pest house reeking with the germs of fatal diseases.

The dangers of alcohol

A second danger arises from frequenting nightclubs, discos, and bars where risqué jokes and too many drinks are the chief menu. The whole atmosphere is diametrically opposed to the preservation of innocence and chastity. Drinking is dangerous, even when it's not done in such an atmosphere. It tends to remove those delicate inhibitions which conscience rears as a protective hedge around one's virtue. While a single drink might not hurt too much, here again we must say that complete abstinence is the wiser and safer course during courtship.

A couple striving to realize their dream of conjugal happiness is struggling for a great prize. Surely the winning of that prize is worth the little act of self-denial involved in abstinence from alcohol. That demon has slain its thousands and its tens of thousands. A couple encountering all the dangers and temptations inherent in courtship will be well advised to give alcohol a wide berth.

Kissing prudence goodbye

A third danger arises from the custom of the good-night kiss. If modest, reverent, and void of passion, it's innocent of all blame. Yet, like all kisses between a man and woman, it's fraught with danger. If prolonged a trifle, passion will swiftly enter. A pleasant evening together can be quickly spoiled. Instead of feeling the exultant joy of a good conscience, with precious memories of the hours spent together, both will feel the stab of an accusing conscience and the instant destruction of their peace of mind.

Women, less susceptible than men to the physical stimuli of sex, and blessed with greater innocence, often fail to perceive the danger in kissing. Men more frequently recognize its peril. Yet it's fraught with hazards for both. Everyone in close touch with courting couples recognizes the threat to self-control which this familiarity presents.

"Ninety percent of the vilest sins of impurity," comments Father William J. Bowdern, S. J., "and that is a conservative estimate — have had their beginning in kisses."[2] The subject is a delicate one. Yet any treatment which seeks to be helpful must come to grips with this potent danger to chastity. Ignorance is not bliss. It's a thousand times better to be forewarned and forearmed.

All who value their honor and their virtue will either forego the good-night kiss altogether or else they'll engage in it with the reverence and respect with which they'd want their own sister to be treated in this regard. Let them remember that God is the third party in all their company and that His eye is upon them as they part.

It should also be mentioned that when a man escorts a woman to the door of her home, he should bid her good night there and never enter. To do so at a late hour, when the other members of the family have retired, is to subject each other to substantially the same danger as the empty apartment or parked car. The failure to observe this rule of elementary prudence has brought heartache and distress to many couples. Only God knows how many pure relationships have been ruined, how many friendships broken up, through the failure to heed this caution.

The call to purity is a call to happiness

By placing these danger signs along the paths of courtship, no one is trying to play the role of killjoy, robbing love of its innocent pleasures, its bright laughter, its hours of happiness. These boundaries merely safeguard a couple's deepest and most enduring happiness, steering them away from the quagmire and quicksand in which they and all their eager hopes and dreams would sink beyond recall. These danger signs on the trails of courtship are like the signs placed upon a road winding along a mountain precipice. Tourists can't ignore even one of them without paying a *big* price.

When these danger signals are faithfully observed, courtship is a time of clean joy and radiant happiness. Each loved one is filled with gladness at the very sight of the other. Conversation has a new relish. Hidden treasures of personality come into view. Lust has not been permitted to creep into the place of innocence and beauty.

A courtship filled with reverence as well as love is a protection for both parties. Leaving one another, a young man and woman should be able to walk to the communion rail to receive with reverent minds and chaste hearts their Eucharistic Lord. To the King of love they should bring their greatest treasure — their own pure love. With ears attuned to His words, they'll then catch His whispering: "Blessed are the pure of heart, for they shall see God." Thus human love can serve as the golden ladder, as seen in Jacob's vision, upon which they may climb to the feet of God, to see His beauty and to taste His sweetness.

The big test

Since God is love, those who have the greatest capacity for pure love may penetrate most deeply into the mystery of His being. Love in man is "above all his works." It's the noblest act of the soul. "'You shall love the Lord your God with all your heart, and with all your soul, and with all your mind, and with all your strength.' This is the first commandment. The second is this, 'You shall love your neighbor as yourself.' There is no other commandment greater than these." (Mark 12:30-32). Love is therefore the fulfillment of the Law.

Where chaste love permeates courtship, it becomes an aid to virtue and a stimulus to holiness. If a couple upon parting for the night feels closer to God in reverence and love, their courtship is one around which angels are hovering. Let each person returning from an evening together listen carefully to the voice of conscience. If it's joyous and exultant, that courtship is good and clean. If it's sad, remorseful, or accusing, then something is wrong in the courtship, something that must be rectified at once or else the relationship must cease. That's the decisive test. Make no mistake about it.

Safeguarding your greatest treasure

While the avoidance of dangerous occasions is an enormous help, a positive love of chastity and an appreciation for its merit are of utmost importance. When one treasures something deeply, he will struggle desperately to retain it. "For where your treasure is," says Christ, "there will your heart be also" (Matthew 6:21). It is well for men and women to prize their treasure of chastity as the pearl of great price, the jewel that is richer than everything else they possess.

No taboos will safeguard chastity if one does not properly value it as a great treasure. This determination to guard chastity must get *into the bloodstream* and become the prime consideration in all actions which involve it.

Chastity must prompt one to say: "Why expose myself to the danger of arousing my passions? Why put my treasure out on the borderline of danger where it may be trampled and disfigured? Why take a chance with something so precious? It isn't worth it. I'll play it safe. If I had a valuable watch I wouldn't leave it on a bench in the mall. I'd keep it safely away from the danger zone. I'll do the same with the greatest treasure I have."

The highest form of love

We must bear in mind that the capacity to love comes from God. Man can't destroy that capacity without dehumanizing himself, without destroying the noblest faculty of his soul. Therefore, since we're compelled by our very nature to love, the remedy for an evil love lies in detaching the will from an unworthy object and in turning it to a deserving one.

What about those, however, who are not courting someone? What about the thousands of single people who will never have the shield of matrimony or a spouse to whom they can pour out the love of their hearts? Are they to suppress their love? On the contrary, they're to direct it to the most worthy recipient — our Lord and Savior, Jesus Christ. He is supremely worthy of their love, and will reciprocate with a generosity which surpasses that of any human lover. In the lifting of our love from a human to a divine Lover, we are transforming, beautifying, and strengthening it.

In substituting Christ for man, we're not frustrating love. We're *elevating* it. This is the supreme and final remedy. Even those who are married will find that, in raising their love to Christ, that which flows over to their partner is but the sweeter. Strong, personal love for Jesus Christ in the Blessed Sacrament is for young and old, for single and married. It's the unfailing bulwark of protection for unspoiled chastity.

Powerful aids to purity

While the preservation of chastity calls for a constant and determined battle, we know that we're not struggling on our own. God's grace is always ready and willing to help us. "God is faithful, and he will not let you be tempted beyond your strength," says St. Paul, "but with the temptation will also provide the way of escape, that you may be able to endure it" (1 Corinthians 10:13). With God's all-powerful help, we can win every victory.

Among the mighty aids which our Holy Faith offers us is devotion to the Blessed Virgin Mary, the Immaculate Mother of God. The daily recitation of the Rosary will prove a rich investment. Every man and woman sincerely desirous of preserving his or her chastity will say each day at least three Hail Marys for this intention. Make that a rule of your life.

Another powerful help is frequent, even daily, reception of Holy Communion. What could bring greater strength and courage to the person struggling against the lusts of the flesh than the reception of Jesus Christ, the Source of all purity and the Author of all chastity? From His throne in the tabernacle, Christ is stretching forth His arms and offering the sweet invitation: "Come to me, all who labor and are heavy laden, and I will give you rest" (Matthew 11:28). The spread of the practice of daily Holy Communion in our land is certain evidence that legions of couples will keep their banners waving high in triumph and will never taste defeat. Make it a practice to receive Holy Communion daily, or at least every Sunday.

The fervent practice of religion, attendance at daily Mass, the cultivation of willpower through little acts of self-denial, the custody of the senses, the avoidance of dangerous occasions, the counsel of one's regular confessor (and everyone should have one), the shepherding of one's thoughts, the reading of good books, the companionship of virtuous friends, and frequent recourse to God in prayer — all these together constitute an unfailing recipe for victory. Have confidence in God and in the power of prayer. Without Christ we can do nothing. With Him, and in Him, we can do all things.

I can do all things in him who strengthens me. – Philippians 4:13

Conclusion:
The Supreme Achievement

The building of a stable home where peace, joy and love abide constitutes the supreme achievement in life. No other enterprise can compare with it in importance, both to the individual and to society. Neither can success in any other field, in business or politics, in social or professional life, act as a substitute for failure in the home. A man may amass a fortune, or he may achieve prominence in his profession. But neither of these achievements can obscure his failure in that undertaking of supreme importance, the building of an enduring and happy home. Fame and loneliness are sorry substitutes for domestic happiness.

Popularity is fickle. Wealth is a sham that turns to dust and ashes. Beauty is what the Irish call a gift from the old lady's left hand; it vanishes to where no leprechaun can find it. Political prominence means teetering for a moment on the precipice before you fall into an abyss.

In contrast, enduring happiness is achieved by the man and woman who build a stable home. The Church offers guidance and help to men and women in the achievement of this great enterprise. Follow the specifications of the Divine Architect of the Christian home, and you can't fail. Make that home one and indissoluble, a generous wellspring of life, not a morgue of frustration and death. Make it a training school of virtue, a shrine of holiness, where souls grow daily into a closer likeness of Christ. Make it a house of God where the table becomes an altar and the fireplace a sanctuary lamp, where the Rosary, frequent Holy Communion, and evening prayers are a family ritual.

Where that divine guidance is followed, you will not be groping in the darkness but clasping the hand of God. And where God is, there is life and light and love; there is Heaven. To the educators, statesmen and social planners who are searching for an answer to the ills that beset our land, I say: put God into the homes of America. To the fathers and mothers who are groping for the path to enduring peace and love and happiness, I say: put God into your home and keep Him there — and all will be well with you and with America.

Endnotes

Chapter 2: Putting Prudence into Practice
[1] *Religion Outlines for Colleges*, Course IV (Washington, D.C.: Catholic Education Press, 1928), p. 103.

Chapter 3: Passion & Purity
[1] Encyclical *On Christian Marriage*, p. 6

[2] *Problems of Courtship and Marriage* (St. Louis: Queen's Work, 1939), p. 18.

Resources

For any of the resources below visit www.familylifecenter.net
You can also call 1-800-705-6131

Catalog

The Family Life Center offers a *free* catalog of a wide selection of tapes, books, and videos on courtship, marriage, faith, family life, and fatherhood. You can also order all items in our online catalog at www.dads.org, or at www.familylifecenter.net.

Conferences

The Family Life Center holds conferences throughout North America. For a *free* list of upcoming men's conferences and courtship conferences, visit either of our Web sites. The Family Life Center also sponsors and participates in conferences for couples on marriage, parenting, homeschooling, faith, and family life. To bring a conference to your community, call us for an information pack.

Just for Men

Most men make the mistake of waiting until their first child arrives to learn the skills of fatherhood. Start learning about fatherhood *now*. The earlier you begin preparing for fatherhood, the more effective a father you'll be. Check out these resources:

- **www.dads.org** is a Web site loaded with free materials for Christian husbands and fathers.
- Subscribe to a free **dads.org e-newsletter** published monthly by Steve Wood at **www.dads.org**.

1. Catholic Courtship: A Challenge to Teens & Twenties,* Steve Wood & Guests
This tape series is a collection of our best live radio interviews on courtship. Includes a real-life courtship story. *3 Tape Album:* $19.95 (F517)

2. Honorable Courtship,* Steve Wood
This best-selling tape answers the question *"What is Courtship?"* and shows you how to implement courtship in your family. *Single Tape*: $7.00 (C148)

3. Date...or Soul Mate? Neil Clark Warren
This book tells you how to know if someone is worth pursuing in 2 dates or less and outlines what increases happiness in marriage. 184pp. *Book:* $10.99 (B370)

4. ABCs of Choosing a Good Husband Live Interviews, Steve Wood
The practical and insightful advice on how to make a wise choice in a marriage partner that Wood shares on these tapes is available nowhere else. Learn how to find *lasting* happiness and contentment in marriage. *6 Tape Album*: $34.95 (C184)

5. Our Marriage Covenant & Our Covenant with God, Steve Wood
This tape illustrates how viewing your marriage covenant in light of your covenant with God will radically transform your marriage. *Single Tape:* $7.00 (C132)

6. Natural Family Planning vs. Birth Control, Steve Wood & Guests
Learn the differences between NFP and birth control, how it affects your marriage, and what the Church teaches. *2 Tape Album:* $14.95 (F508)

7. Building Your Marriage on the Rock,* Steve Wood
This best-selling album covers how to build a strong and lasting marriage, how to overcome marriage conflicts, and more. *2 Tape Album:* $14.95 (C115)

8. Raising the Standard in Our Marriages, Steve Wood
Learn the seven Scriptural "secrets" to a happy marriage, how to rekindle love in marriage, how to avoid money conflicts, and more. *Single Tape:* $7.00 (C142)

9. Catholic Handbook for Engaged & Newly Married Couples, Frederick Marks
This is one of the best marriage guidebooks ever. 154pp. *Book:* $9.95 (B370)

*These titles are also available on CD. See our online catalog.
Family Life Center - 22226 Westchester Blvd. - Port Charlotte, FL 33952
Orders: (800) 705-6131 - Fax: (941) 743-5352 - E-mail: mail@familylifecenter.net

Courtship & Marriage Resources

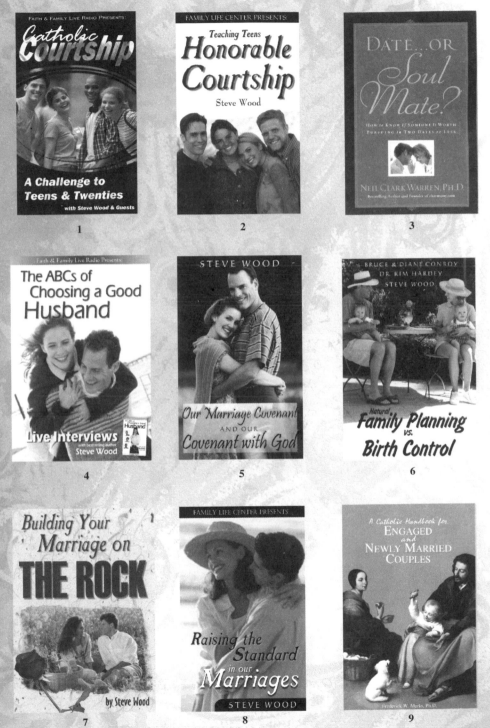

Finally, a guidebook for making the most important decision of your life.

Finding a good spouse is no easy task in our materialistic, pleasure-seeking, divorce-plagued society. These unique new books offer practical and insightful advice on how to choose a partner for life.

Topics covered include:
- Key questions to ask before getting married
- How to develop good communication skills
- How to know when you've met the person you want to marry
- How to avoid getting stuck in dead-end relationships
- Two reliable ways to determine if your relationship has the potential for a lasting marriage
- When are you ready to marry?
- The answer to the common question, "How far can we go before marriage?"

$12.95 per copy + $2.95 S/H (U.S. orders)

Family Life Center - 22226 Westchester Blvd - Port Charlotte, FL 33952
(800) 705-6131 - Fax: (941) 743-5352 - www.familylifecenter.net

About the Author

Rev. John A. O'Brien, Ph.D.
1893 - 1980

Until his death in 1980, Rev. John A. O'Brien was a professor of the Philosophy of Religion at the University of Notre Dame. He authored dozens of books on philosophy, religion and the sciences, and was a popular Catholic apologist whose books, articles, and pamphlets have reached millions. Fr. O'Brien was a founder of the Newman Club movement, and was also a leading evangelist of his time.

Born January 20, 1893 in Peoria, Illinois, John A. O'Brien attended Holy Cross College (Worcester, Massachusetts), and St. Viator's College (Bourbonnais, Illinois). He was ordained to the priesthood by Bishop Edmund Dunne in 1916. He served as chaplain for the Catholic students at the University of Illinois for 22 years and earned a Ph.D. in psychology there. He started the Newman Foundation at the University of Illinois.

For the rest of his life Fr. O'Brien taught and wrote at the University of Notre Dame. Fr. O'Brien believed that Catholics ought to work actively to convert others to the Catholic faith; thus, he participated in crusades to that end, organized campaigns in 50 American dioceses, spent his summers preaching in the streets of southern cities, published articles in popular magazines, and wrote pamphlets to promote missionary efforts and explain the doctrines of the Catholic Church.

Fr. O'Brien wrote 45 books and hundreds of pamphlets and articles. In 1973, the University of Notre Dame awarded him the Laetare Medal. He died April 18, 1980, in South Bend, Indiana.